Diversities of Silence

CW00819738

Diversities of Silence

DAPHNE GLOAG

Brentham Press

First published 1995 by
Brentham Press 40 Oswald Road, St Albans, Herts AL1 3AQ

ISBN 0 905772 45 8

British Library Cataloguing–in–Publication Data
A catalogue record for this book is available from the British Library

Cover design: Harmonograph by David Williamson

Printed in England by Watkiss Studios Ltd, Biggleswade, Beds SG18 9ST

For Peter, who shares poetry with me; and in memory of my mother, who led me to it, and of my father

Contents

Acknowledgments

Some of these poems have been published in *Ambit, English, Litmus, New Poetry, Outposts,* and *Wheels;* in *Poems from the Medical World* (edited by Howard Sergeant) and *Contemporary Women Poets* (edited by Trevor Kneale); and among prizewinning poems from Bridport and York Poetry competitions. Some have been broadcast on BBC Radio Three (*Poetry Now*) and Radio London. "The Mosaics of Cefalù" is being published in an Italian translation in the Palermo journal *Segno.*

THE MOUNTAIN

1

There is just the mountain staring,
its peak penetrating the sky.
The uncertain summit taunts our hours.
Drei Stunde says the notice;
three hours we wonder, as the alpine accentor
slips on the air its slight song.

Our experience is not
of the rock blazing.
Light has flowered in our meadows,
the spacious gloss of day has hovered
above gentians, asters, orchids,
above mountains diminished under the sun.
We do not know
sharp rock sparking against stretched limbs,
sparks of the sun igniting the rock edge.
Easy paths have held our boots;
forests were slack on known slopes.
We do not know
sun swollen in the sky,
sky out of control.

We reach a lake curling at the mountain's foot.
Here the mountain has come down from the sky
and the sun lies safe in blue water.
We need not be blinded by the sun or the forked rock:
we can cope with reflections.
We need not see the snow blazing.

2

My companions abandon the mountain
fearing the black rock rising.
No ease of the earth distracts here
from bared rock and the final snow.

Zwei oder drei schreckliche Momente,
say the climbers. Before the first bad moment
I meet an Austrian family. *Ganz allein...*

9

I arrange slow phrases, they accept me;
we eat dates and exchange names with spare words.
Then our route hesitates above the cliff drop.
But here abyss means acceptable danger,
the light shrieking.

The boy with long thin limbs clambers out of sight;
they call him, his name flies round the mountain.
But he in his safe nonchalence finds
the rocks marked with reassuring red.

Improbable glacier buttercups startle the dark rock.
I have here at last
the rock itself,
igneous mountain cooled from the fiery earth,
and out of the intense core
the slow crystals of the urgent slope
and the final snow
blazing.

THE SMOOTH HILL

This kind of achievement has its limitations,
you say: one perfectly rounded smooth green hill,
two trees on its side bowed horizontal by the wind and
two round pink clouds grazing its summit.

It is an uneventful perfection, not torn from travail
or pieced together precariously: a calm legato
not probing pains or leading to visions
but leaving certainty and a seed of stillness.

I have sought rather for the ragged uncertain peak
not perfectly known and mastered improbably,
having complexity of riches or none. But this hill
is here to be climbed in the late sun.

RAVEN

The raven with its not quite musical call
filling the wide mist
lists in the gale and is tossed
and is yet the gale's equal
above the hill's highest rock:
prruk prruk – a clock
wound with its rusty key that will last for ever.

Wind is hard,
wind and rocks cut;
muscle filaments slide, pull on ratchet;
wind and muscle clash. The bird
just not dashed
against reeling rock is pushed
to the summit of the wind's high violence.

BUZZARDS

If, flinging off limbs and plodding,
we took on the flight of the far buzzard
what would we do with that mastery of sky, circling,
surveying summits, riding the rhetoric of winds?

I in such extremity of air
with wing tip feathers accurately upturning
would seek your longed for space, always making
an absorbed counterpoint of circling wings.

As it is we have our hugger mugger space;
touching touching we push past despotic minutes.
At last the quiet lines of hills amaze
our hearts and the infinite air surrounds us.

THE SKIES OF VINCENT VAN GOGH

1
The Sower (1888)

Spare taut lines
are the economy of the year;
the colours are
dead earth.

The man's range is narrow
and concentrated;
his body swings
seed to the open soil.

A blown bent tree
twists towards the earth,
brown inert leaves
splayed on branches.

But the sun, huge drum,
sounds over the sky:
one sky can hardly hold
the whole sun.

Over the sky branches
draw great arcs,
templates for huger suns,
with a dead twig in the sun's circle.

Furrows drive to the edge
of the sky, all tracks converge
at the rim of the world
below the sun.

Earth has no end;
horizon touches the sun,
sun touches the sower's head.
Seed will come to grain.

2
Starry Night (1889)

No pale contrivance of the stars
could so rivet the night,
but he drawing out from the cosmos
inexhaustible skeins of light
fixes to the sky all brilliances.

Two cypresses gather spirals of darkness
while the moon eddies in light –
no passive reflector, satellite
of a planet, but author of brightness
spinning yellow rays. A tension

of lights and darknesses holds the eye;
day and night are together
in a sky without end in the universe,
where he finally will quench
the dark with his authentic suns.

CREATION
God creates Adam in a painting by Blake

A too explicit strength might lay him low
before life has started, leave him
wasted, strangled, a struggling shadow
stretched on the green swell of the unending ocean.
The wings flatten him, the absorbed power.

Can he ever lie at peace below that brutal
bulging cloud and the flung red
swords of light? Limbs are pulled, constricted,
neck twisted; his eyes concentrate
on a far stretched pain or doom.

But the stretching shape laid over him
becomes his shape and the world grows in space,
an extremity of darkness and light exploding.

DANTE IN THE EMPYREAN DRINKING AT THE RIVER OF LIGHT
A watercolour by Blake

I was disappointed, expecting colour
for the River of Light. I said,
Perhaps the light has faded. But you
said each person must make his own colour.
I will paint it purple, silver and red.

But colour is not the point. You drink from rivers
when shrivelled with fiery thirst,
revive drooping limbs with water and coolness,
splash the stooping mind with light.
The water shines and is colourless.

The river has sound not colour.
There are the bright trumpets of light,
drums reverberate, the crescendo comes,
its light crashes with a valour
of percussion to its climax in the mind.

The River of Light flows
without inhibition, prodigal
and powerful. Flow and fluency
are the point; the drinker grows
in his dazzle of daring.

DEPTHS

...ad ora ad ora
m'insegnavate come l'uom s'etterna – Dante*

No you can't see it anywhere here –
and why should you expect it?
But looking down
you see strips and snakes of light where
the sea ripples, and humps of shadow.
Then there are the colours:
gradations of turquoise, intrusions of blue,
down and down
drawing the mind with the ardour of sight,
water grabbing light,
sight greedy to grasp and own, a gate
perhaps to break through.

But sitting here discussing the Italian for "last straw"
or walking along chatting about life
we think this is the real thing:
it's where we are at, here
together;
it's what we can't get enough of,
brainstorming our way from night to day.
We watch a lizard dash for a crack
in the rock,
and another emerge from the rock's black depths.

Jacob wrestled all night with God and saw
his face before the day broke.
We have easier assignations with symbols of the eternal.
Rock and water we see
everywhere, and lucidities more persuasive than logic.

---

*From *Inferno* XV: "...hour by hour you taught me how man
makes himself eternal"

Jacob dreamed of a ladder between earth and heaven.
Ladders can go up or down, starting anywhere,
from any random rush of being or the quiet
sea—wet sand under the moon.
From the jetty we look down
and see blue and silver skipper fish
darting through light.

WINCHESTER CATHEDRAL NAVE

After the years without
this rising of light and stone
I stood seeing quiet perpendiculars,
the lines of light,
the final fountain of stone.

In contained elation the columns rose,
at last exploding
into an intricate sky where rays
of stone were knotted and held
in light's eventual crown.

All lines connected in the stone
in this élan of height,
this rush of stone and light.
There will be space in the years
for lines breaking into fans of life.

In the dark I saw the nave again
when the stone screen was lit,
a sole and total light.
To catch my train I hurried out
remembering light that would fit in my cupped hands.

THE MOSAICS OF CEFALÙ, SICILY

"Can heaven be like this?" I said,
as we entered the Norman cathedral
stunned by the gold and the glory.
From the high point of the mosaics
the eyes of Jesus hold us;
his right hand points upwards,
his left hand has words of life:
I am the light of the world;
whoever follows me shall not walk in darkness
but shall have the light of life.

But what has gold to do with it,
or the high up glory of it all?
Do the people sitting on balconies
with the washing hanging out to dry
in narrow streets with their sky a rationed strip
want kilos of gold to lead them to heaven?

Will the bride leaving the cathedral,
with her train a kilometre long
billowing briefly in sea wind on the jetty
before she meets her births and deaths,
be helped by all this gold?

Are the street kids of Palermo
lit by the gold of Monreale,
or by the quiet work of the parish priest
murdered last week by the Mafia?
With tears in their eyes they say,
"We played with him the game of 'who laughs first'
and he gave us festas and lots of good things to eat,
but now he's gone."

And yet the imperative
of that high gold of Jesus Christ
tries to grasp us: we grope
to take it into our dark depths.
The cathedral grows dark;
a stone angel casts a shadow on the wall.
But the sunset strikes imperious light
from the mosaic cherubim.
The light moves slowly.
Another day perhaps
it will reach us.

THREE MEN'S JOURNEY

1
Pieces of the day
are lost   we look
for completion

waiting also for that bright conjunction of planets
swinging in the night

We wait always
for what may never come

2
We hide from the sky
in deep woods where sound
is the drop of leaves

Black leaves
muffle the ground
snuff out our steps

We hide
from the sky's wide ageless eye

3
Seasons are in abeyance
We avoid
the roads of the sky

There is scaffolding of branches
against the clouds
trees congest space

But it will be possible at last
when the wood fades

to find where the open sky flows

LIT STONE
In Durham Cathedral

This is our marriage, you said
in that kingdom of massed stone,
where light was the voices rising

and anthems were sunlight piercing
Norman arches, pointing
to chiselled chevrons and the vast

girth of granite. *I will love you
to the end of life*, you said,
and afterwards. Shaken

by lifted music and the lit stone
we left the cathedral, speaking
of the chapter house's ancient glass:

the bird's head (*our bird*, you said),
yellow grass seeding, and a fragment
of a man on a cross raised.

WINGS

Wings what are wings about? I say,
gazing at the angel of Simone Martini.

Looking from gold to gold
we see the upstretched hand and serene arch
of wings point Mary, recoiling a little now
at that hard annunciation, to the unthought of
ecstasy (we content with gold
and the light of lilies).

Looking up from the page we see
the swifts are flying, their high wings
flowing through the ease of the day,
air their element,
their feeding ground and rest,
the fluent curve of wings their mastery.

Wings wings are the high content of the day:
we share this day of wings.

PRECISIONS

So accurately the trunk's tip grasps
a clump of grass, delicately
rolling up just far enough
then without haste swinging
the morsel to the vast mouth.

Loving the precision we touch
each other's fingertips. Such calm
and almost grace as the thick feet
slowly step across the dust
move us. We discuss the great

flaps of ears as the elephant flicks
her trunk to the barrier alert
in air. Has she really grabbed
cameras and bags as the notice warns? We
love each other wondering and absorbed.

THE VISIT
Children born after their mothers had a kidney transplant
meet the Minister at the zoo

The camels might never have been here.
They stand tall and indifferent
while the children climb between their humps.
The government minister holds a baby; mothers
are almost blooming and carefree. They possess the day.
Minister, Minister, shout the photographers,
look this way please. Camels dying
in deserts are far and forgotten nearly.

Beyond the zoo wind tangles
in precarious grass, temporary daffodils
are suddenly remarkable. The day of camels,
warm camel breath, and the ugly convenient humps
are irreplaceable. A moon faced mother,
amused, absorbed, holds up her child
to the camel's brown, comfortable hair,
straggling, undeniable.

A VIEW OF BEETHOVEN'S LATE QUARTETS
In memory of FC

It is done often,
pushing beyond the limits
of standing stones:

so our ancestors
went from the round hill in the sun
and ritual circles

to carved columns
and the spires piercing cloud;
and now trailing a vast fire

spacecraft leave earth.
What is unique
is this particular daring

of never before climbed
peaks and jagged ridges.
The provisional path

questions the aspect
of the far sky,
clouds hold their usual rain

in new configurations,
and the unknown air
is a rare element.

OAK GALL
For my father

Driving through the Welsh mountains
this afternoon of October twilight
mesmerised by breath and heartbeat
and the hills' moving outline –
he quietly hoping he'll reach eighty
and I with my life perhaps half over –
suddenly we reach a more palpable darkness,
bracken and birches poised before night
and ahead the last lap of the sky's light.

We drive wrapped in the world's silence
not speaking of the turning earth or
variable sun. An ash tree places
spread hands against the sky, a blackness;
air shivers. The moment swelling
like an oak gall feeds and shelters
this small sense of death and love. Driving
towards home we rest in the serenity of breath
accepting day and day's loss and the dying earth.

YOUR SEA
A sonnet for my mother

The sea has all persuasions. You have seen
the first still morning of the created earth
poised in a frail floating mist between
horizon and sea's edge. The sun's lit path
lay on the water, leading to who knows
what secret islands of the world. And there
you have danced at the high tide, the massing rise
of waters gathered with huge forces where
the cliffs are battlemented and the spray's
dense volleys pound the rocks with unfailing fire
from the waves' most thunderous armoury. The days
of the spring tide will come again with power
of breaking waters and again the sea
will be before you in immensity.

THALES OF MILETUS

In Miletus men looked beyond
their bread, and the sun at night
was beyond the Ionian Sea
and their confident ships of oil and corn
travelled the path of the sun,
halcyon birds skimming the waves before them.

Thales the philosopher
sat beneath the shifting wind.
What is the world? he asked;
*What stuff is the world made of
that stays through the wrack of seasons
and the flux of the earth?*

Below him the sea rounded to a wave
and splintered on the white headland.
World of water, all things are water –
black earth, heavy cornfields of the coastlands,
vineyards heavy with wine:
water the first of elements.

To men at ease in the evening asking,
All things are full of gods, he said,
as they looked for the departing ships,
as the migrating hawks crossed the moon,
full of the universal element,
he said as olive leaves disturbed the night.

The sea was there always.
This is worst, when sea is lost.

LUCRETIUS AND THE PIGEON IN THE PARK

It is only a plump grey bird,
greedy with breadcrumbs,
and here on the broad
grass it has no dove-like nature.

But Lucretius wrote
of the feathers of its throat and neck
changing under the light.
These shifting purples and greens

told him the primary particles
had no colour
but depended on the light.
The world's elements wait

for colour: all things
are possible. But as the bird
struts in the park
I, passing November roses, walk

to an office where all things
are not possible, where lands
of invention are reduced to minutes,
and I cannot innovate ends.

But here the bird will fly, all birds
are flying, green is purple,
crescents of purple are flying, all
colours, words, days are possible.

A SUDDEN TURBULENCE

Seeing has a way of sudden
turbulence, an amazement of the light.
I have seen in an unbidden
movement of an ordered day
hidden purple sheen on heads
of tufted ducks. For all my life
they have been only black and white,
and now this subtle grace of sight
from the grey city path by the winter lake.

It might go no further: curves of cloud
and intricate traffic as the clock strikes
deflect eyes and resonances, I heeding
only scraps and ends of memory, folding
miles and minutes into tidy packages.
But echoes gather. Reaching my place of work
I climb the dark staircase. Echoes are here
unnoticed. But at the top I will hear them sometimes, finding
unfolded shutters and seeing below the fountain flying.

FLORESTAN IN HIS DUNGEON

Green air once
was my sufficient day
(swallows flying flying
owning the sky)

A ship sailed once   the ample wind held voices
the wake ran with quicksilver
Now the dark is hard
solid cold scabs the skin

Three red petals spreadeagled on the face of the moon
the abject light falls twitters away
the petals fold and blanch
the most immense night waits

Floor walls creep on me cold stone
the dark stares at me   I will slash those eyes of night
then the dark will be bright with blood   fires
will leap up   stabbing lights

The cold stone is all
Is death so cold   dead
flesh so rigid? My blood
stops its rivers here

Elsewhere it is autumn
the clouds compose themselves
The last yellow leaf at the top of my birch tree
would splinter my eyes with its uncontrollable light

NO LOOKED FOR DAY

It is not the difficult
night that makes
the castaway of the morning.

For it is possible always
to make that one resolved
step into day,

just as the climber,
having reached at length
the last ridge in the mist,

reserves zeal
for the final scaling
of the coveted peak beyond cloud;

this, like the mastering
of difficult rock
with long drawn skill,

is a built in end. Thus
I think more
of the loss of paths

and those who have no
looked for day or summit;
lacking maybe mastery

they yet have no sheer fall,
shouting, from rocks,
or avalanche bringing

repose. It was so
for Prometheus
bringer of fire to man,

who day long was food for vultures
and nightly had his
gnawed liver renewed

for the onslaughts of day.
He, chained to his mountain crag,
saw no end.

NOT A STRAIGHT LINE BETWEEN TWO ROSE BUSHES

Always it is the finest thread, scarcely
to be touched; spiders have a mercy

of moon weight and rose branches are gross
as spacecraft. The most sharp toss

of wind yet leaves the line intact. But this
shortest distance between two points is

banal geometry. The angles of the suspended
web (catching light in the wind) define a needed

complexity. I look for patterns laid
in the intricate light of the predatory thread.

REFLECTIONS ON RADIO TELESCOPES

My interest in the radio telescope
chiefly lies in the
principle on which it works,

collecting radio waves
from a certain direction and
gathering at a single point

dispersed lines. Thus it
concentrates
that which the star or galaxy

has scattered. It bends
all to a focus and
defines wavelength.

It can also turn
in different directions
gathering all that is,

detector and conserver.
Some are beautiful, with slender
intricacies of steel,

white tracery against the sky
supporting huge parabolas
and rising aerials.

It is possible to find
elsewhere this principle.
I in him had proved it,

he who gathered for me
radiations from various sources,
making them intense.

But space is large,
and he discovered for me
also the empty places.

NO DELICACIES OF LIGHT
John Clare in Northampton Asylum

The twenty years are a narrow twisting road
the road is empty and no friends come that way

The nest's moss lined centre
is a hole of nothing not a solitude

It is stuffed with unbelonging faces
a deformed silence

Moss and mud form prison walls
no paths lead to the yellow hyacinth

The celandine's fires have fled
cowslips no longer flower in improbable December

The sky is a black flat dish
holding now no delicacies of light

FLIGHT OF THE REDWING
Visit to a patient in a mental hospital

Redwings pasturing in a brown ploughed field
smart with their white eye stripes and chestnut rumps
flying free in the corridors of the cold.

Also gulls sweeping the sky
with wings bearing the sun, their cry
clear in the thin blue light of winter.

Then a place where the large sky is unavailing,
where the burden of white spaces is a threat,
where walls are a prison to be coveted

for some. But others cry
for the flight of the redwing and for suns
not now to be summoned from the sky.

THE LOST SUN

She has refused injections to kill pain;
they are too painful, she protests, for her fleshless body,
confusing them with the more difficult hurt
of dying alone. Crossing the heath I visit her,
tactlessly with mud on my boots and the glow of wind.
We speak of travel and music and the never coming spring.
One dying in that unnecessary pain
in the unpeopled night
will not cry for the lost sun and irretrievable music

TURNER'S LAST SUN

The sun topples from the bed,
flat light sways,
his earth shrinks.
Always a frame of light
held his world together:
if the sun fails now
all sense fails,
that craft of light is
nothing,
there is a vast night.

Flesh falls,
flesh no swift ship now;
flesh is derided by the escaping sky
as eyeless Polyphemus was by Ulysses.
But at the last
sky returns
with the exploding light of the sun.

Ulysses deriding Polyphemus is a painting by Turner

SILENCE SUSPENDS THE DAY

The jig-jag of the fairground falls,
the big wheel hovers in transient air
(the haunted castle still emitting howls):

a naked moment. Without trappings
I the funny man continue on my way
in my lonely transit camp, my

precise meridian lost.
Banal merry-go-rounds canter best,
a necessary accompaniment

to the banality of breath.
The wooden horse has an always raised hoof,
solid certainty flowing from his curled mane.

But once silence suspends the day
I gulp the wind seeking my vacant hat.
Children win goldfish that will soon die,

frayed clouds eat at the sun.
But the coconuts are real, they say,
and candyfloss remains shocking pink.

Families enact compulsory fun
(the haunted castle cannot create fears
with synthesised screams and roars).

They do not notice me.
Hot dogs and hamburgers console, "The Skaters' Waltz"
continues. They do not see

streamers strangling air, the weight
of vacancy above my head cutting off
my crimson consciousness before night.

THE CAVE OF EILEITHYIA, CRETE

The cave is empty.
The world turns here
in the dark. The rock
hangs and drips. The lost goddess
was here convenient
to all need of birth, rich once
in immense earth.

The mind hears its own beat;
windless cold grabs
the skin. The cave pulls our steps
away from the fig tree in the sun.
Feet try routes through the wet rock.
Candles pulse weakly, make
no roads in the dark.

The last white spear of light
is cast away. I seek
my dark being and the womb of thought
where the darkness was fertile once.
But the squat clay idols are lost now,
the stalagmite is no longer sacred; only
questions thrust in the dark.

FAUSTUS
Glutted now with learning's golden store – Marlowe

1
Faustus holds the names of all things
(he watches his lack,
closing shutters against the eyes of the day):
knowing all names
he lacks the world.
Earth is dried, sea dead,
sky cold.

His lack gapes:
he reads hearing his own heart beat,
piled hoard of books lying at fingertip,
dust an irrelevance.
He watches his mind,
living no longer in the abundant wind.

He knows all names;
omens not visions wait,
planets move elliptical
at the edge of knowing:
by no straight route
is the end reached.

His lack gapes
(clouds clouds following always the sun),
requiring another dispensation of the universe.

2
He sees the uncovered bones
of wise men; the ebb tide ends
in dry sand, all books are trash.
Is the sea–race of possessed ecstasy
in the swash and backwash of the tides?
In an arrested time when seasons do not strive
the adequate hour waits.
Which of the world's ways leads to the last ocean,
where waves spread far beneath the sky,
covering at length all dry places?

Philosophy and law
he sees as threads
of a screw:
the universe
is not fixed
by their turning.

To heal the sick
is not to cancel
the doom of flesh:
no physician can restore
the stopped brain.

Theology is a land
of no harvest,
its seeds infertile
lacking the wind
of the world. God
does not walk there.

All professions are tawdry toys that grown men play with.
But now he has within him the perfect circle
and all incantations.
Faustus, student of the universe,
with passionate knowledge will conquer the cosmic spheres.

Memories howl before dawn.
The burning comet dissipates its promise
in the unheard of territory of night.

3
He turns from the bland face of the sun,
that old deceiver of men.
Here reeds and leaves are shredded rags
sodden in the black river;
matted grass drapes low twigs of sallow,
the junk of the old year.
Yet the sun is caught piecemeal
in the clotted tangle of the water:
fragments are reflected, sending
fire along the maze of weed.

There is no escape from the sparks of that old perfection
among the flippant fireworks of the Devil's spells.

Last year's seeds fly
from the immoderate cudgel of the bulrush;
a heron wading at the river's edge
moves to target for accurate and swift kill.
Barges pass carrying unseen cargo to the black horizon,
the river flowing without check.
There is no spring of green flutes:
the earth cracks,
dark spring of drums,
when Mephistopheles, his dreaded, desired one, is come.
Birth call and death call are one.

4
Mephistopheles ploughs the parts of knowledge,
answers all questions,
brings books for all needs,
star charts and floras and books of chemistry.
He knows names without end,
Mephistopheles the cheap conjuror.

Yet there are for breaking
the far walls of the mind.
Faustus sees what rising rock to cling to;
he will know the paths of planets
and remote expansions of galaxies.
Sky is endless.

Who made the world? Faustus cries;
but the Devil shrinks from that glory.

5
Through no known gate
he goes to his black harvest.
Circles of sky seed vastly,
his burning intellect presses to climax,
voluptuousness of mind not quenched;

but sometimes seen
the pit before him gapes,
his sought prize a wind gone.

Such contracts for a soul.
The final fear of grabbing fiend
sapping will
snaps the thin thread of sight,
his all of being
wraps in the pall of hell,
he wishing his soul a small blown smoke.
Across empty air
a huge doom sounds.

ST JEROME TRANSLATES THE BIBLE FROM GREEK INTO LATIN
A copperplate engraving by Dürer

Through the high window
light streams
from the ample sky,
the chiaroscuro day:

medallions
of sun are thrown
through the windows' roundels
on stone of walls and mullions.

Bared bone,
a skull
lies on the sill;
death is accommodated here,

and pain:
the God
dying on a cross
confronts the man.

But the room is rich
and used –
tasselled cushions
not too precisely placed,

slippers lying careless;
beads and books await
their own hour,
time not of the hour glass.

Hanging contained on the wall
is the huge brimmed hat:
in accepted toil
it has given shadow.

The hanging gourd
dried
to serve the man
keeps its leaves and tendrils.

Animals cause no surprise;
they have their own place.
The wolf like an embryo
sleeps at ease.

The lion, benign,
stretching his paws,
tail curled, lies
with eyes half closed.

But he possesses still
his own nature;
claws are sharp.
The beasts are not diminished here.

The man is absorbed
and filled,
the light is his own,
mind is rich,

his light will not shrink:
all light
converges here
at the point where

possessed silence
is not a loss
of multitude
but a bright wholeness.

DIVERSITIES OF SILENCE
Three days in an infectious diseases unit

1
The bed has a bright orange counterpane
floor length curtains are blue and green and white
but the room is furnished with emptiness

Silence lies in wait for me
the humming ceiling filter isolates my breath
amplifying silence
walls are white white
the glass will not shatter
Others also are isolated
by the bars of silence
It is not permitted me to know
what crimes of illness brought them
to this solitary confinement.

My thoughts toll slowly   they have a muffled ring
my negatives are absolute

2
There have been other silences
at the edge of night
sky ribbed with orange light of falling day
black sea surrounding me
earth empty
sudden white light of the mind
seeing the world for the first time
all the blues and greens of the world hanging in the sky
and the orange light
and white waves spilling round my feet
mind world tilting on the edge of light

The ward sister comes from Wales
We talked of lakes hidden in the hills
and a beach where fossils lie exposed
in limestone worn by the spring tides

46

I did not speak
of that shore where darkness and escalating light
hung together in the sky
It was a buried ecstasy

3
Silver trains pass the hospital
The nurse said *I go home that way*
Find out when the trains run
It will give you something to do

I have plenty to do
I have the works of Milton
I read of hell and chaos
here where they fight against hell
and chaos is kept at bay
by the friendly orderly wearing plastic gloves
The trains I discover run every seven minutes
Milton was wrong about chaos
It is not a negative

4
Trains pass and pass
I will return
out of this negligible day
and travel into crowds and worlds
out of this nothing
out of this dormouse space
out of silences
into the rust of cities
where the zero between heartbeats
is erased by the roar of trains
and I will lose again the old silences
and the explosions of the orange sun
falling into night

5
Outside my window is a no man's land of unpaved earth
Here I watch the wildlife of the place
sparrows clothed modestly in shades of brown

pecking for scant seeds
and fluttering in the dust
But it is said that kestrels nested here
mistaking the hospital for their ancestral cliffs
as they hovered holding winds
And now a gull flies twisting in air
the angle of its wings cutting through void sky
the keen edge falling rising
Flight is still possible

6

You should have rung the bell the nurse said
We could have made you tea
But it is enough to know
faces and words are the other side of silence

It is enough to know
I am scooped out and filled
with this emptiness this silence
It could become a buoyancy
carrying me beyond my ordered river
to the chaos of waters
where a canoe shoots the rapids
and is driven by a fire of spray
and the falls are a euphoria
a flying light of the white river

7

The doctor says I'll live to be a hundred
a space of years
years skies leading
faces words leading
to what diversities of silence

I read an article on Thracian treasures
gold and jewels buried through blind years
blank silver hammered into form
On a round plaque lion–griffins and winged lions
are poised and taut   wings are stretched

48

In the centre Hercules struggles with a lion
in calm strength
Possessing their silver circle
the animals lie in wait
for the undeniable sun

8
On the radio
the stripped music climbs and falls
lean phrases of Bach's cello suite
finding the shape of music
flowing through silence

The notes are sparse leaves of autumn
Through them white sky is seen
at first dead space
then the violent silence of moving clouds
and storms racing
They catch also the daytime moon
and they will be the place
of the intensest sun
light's extremity

EASE OF WINGS

Wings are a prosperity
an aplomb of the air
a greed of going

This winter I live
in a city of gulls of wings
the crowded air

is white
I will not hold
dead leaves

Wings are a beseeching
a refusal
of final earth

I too shall find
this ease of wings
and whiteness

ERGO SUM

Not at all times
or over all the sky
are the doves flying

but one white
instant of wings
between

nothing and nothing
sings light
and I am

BUTTERFLIES IN THE NATURAL HISTORY MUSEUM

If it were elsewhere so...perhaps indeed
somewhere on earth they do lie thus beneath
the sun, vivid with no space between
insistent wings.

Here no leaves conceal them or shadows,
no birds feed them to their young.
Here they are not searched for: they are
inevitable.

But my butterflies are found singly
in large winds, and they can fly;
they cannot be pinned down, they
do not demand me.

I must reflect also on this:
it is not, as in the museum, always
butterfly time. There are eggs, a matter of faith,
inconvenient

caterpillars, and the resting pupae.
Only at the end the imago comes,
at first soft and crumpled but soon a butterfly
smooth and shining.

THREE WALLS

One wall where stones are spent in the wind:
repair is ceaseless
and no sky is seen through holes.
All day men come, men go,
finding trinkets for the interstices.
If necessary wallpaper can cover cracks;
we prefer lilies and humming birds to plain stripes.
The wall too is hung with bells
to drown the screech owl in the night.

The second wall a place for the wind to play:
clouds fly through it in storms,
shadows caparison the holes;
the sun may be observed through it at dawn,
also the falling and the rising moon;
and you may discover sometimes
a nest of wrens or stonechats in a hole.
But some years all holes are empty, scoured by the wind,
and the wind is cold and there is nothing.

A third wall nearly solid:
here there is one hole
and inside a shaped stone grown to the gap,
a finished fit, absorbing space,
white stone with its own light
holding all the stresses of the wall,
concentrating strength.
Here at the falling of the day
there are no deficits.

THE LAKE AT EVENING

With the first plump leap of fish I know it.
The rush flowering flows in the wind; tousled
thistle and willowherb tangle together; meadowsweet
is heavy and rich. A cow lows. Swallows and martins
dash and dare, loquacious in flight;
a reed warbler raises a sudden bank of sound.

There is no angularity here, experience
flows. No noise is accident, there are no
idle places. I choose and am, without dissonance.
It is a gathered whole. But where the fish rise
the circles widen wakening the water
and break the reflected willows and the composed sky.

SPACE IS NOT EMPTINESS

Each irrevocable wave falls easily on the sand,
a disintegration natural and complete.

The long lines of foam fill the mind,
they fill the lost centuries reaching back

to archaic seas unchanged. The moving sky
above the winds is total here with no

interrupted lights. Space is not emptiness, high
gulls flow in sunlight. The surface shimmer

touches no terrors; you can walk here
with a child forgetting the harsh crash

of the black waves of storm and black rock faces.
But this refinement of shining and level water

sparks a limitless daring of the open sea;
the complete sky merges

into unrealised waters, shearing
from edges of the known light to an unknown peace.

AT AN EXHIBITION
Treasures from Byzantium

Icon of the Nativity (from Crete, 15th century)

"Come on," you said, "you must look at this one."
The gold of the icon drew us on.

The baby, outside the black gash of a cave,
lies tightly wrapped, watched
by a cow and horse attentive

as Wise Men on their horses bound up the rocks.
But his mother, on a scarlet bed, looks
the other way, at the same infant

about to be bathed below the rock. All times
converge in this intensest season
and disparate ways against reason

are one. A black cross cuts through
the rock, scarcely visible;
the Wise Men's searched-for star

shines from its wood. Angels blaze, singing or bending
towards the manger. This ardent hour
flashes into mortal heeding

as one angel talks to a shepherd. In red
another shepherd plays a flute,
while one seems to gesticulate

to Joseph, thoughtful in his gold robes.
Sheep drink from a stream or nibble branches.
A dog is curled up, a goat scratches

his ear. Ordinary moments are given gold;
fragments of life and liking are crowded
into this small square of gold.

We see nine stars in the sky, sharing the joy.

Treasures from Byzantium

*A pair of silver plates with Dionysiac figures (probably
Eastern Empire, 4th century; from Mildenhall treasure)*

Two circles holding sprung energies beyond words:
two girls dancing with their mantles swirling
into huge circles beyond their heads; one plays on
double pipes, one holds up a tambourine. They are breaking
out of the grey grain of the world, flowing flowing

through music. On one plate Pan, half animal, plays his pipes;
on the other a satyr, half turned towards the girl, dances
with one arm stretched above his head arching grasping
ecstasy: what wine of the world flows through them?
Movement is fluent, they inhabit an unconstrained music.

The pictured pipes and castanets, wand, fruit, and covered
       dishes
are symbols of an ancient vision, the curves of dancing
a betrayed freedom held by the tight bead rims of silver.
Yet a final music flings off the perfected silence, leaping
boundaries, sweeping past all meagre paths of careful thought.

SPRING THE CATACLYSM

The necessary aggression of living cells
multiplying to million millions lies in hiding
in the fragile haze: white wine
having undergone the violence of fermentation
tranquil in a crystal glass. But breaking seeds,
splitting buds, movement of far roots
are the land's cataclysm, thunder
and thrust of growth, the harsh, brash
action of the cell's intricate machinery
leaving the dormant dark for sudden unthinkable suns.

A SUDDEN SPRING

The difficult spring
a raw ghost
and then the amazed growth
    a giddiness in the
    sudden sun

sky a little veiled
by the slight leaves
ducklings risen from their eggs
    love the sudden
    ease of spring

and the hawthorn blossom
conspiring with the sun
on a sudden day
    love the flowering
    of all seasons

WEDDING DAY
Sonnet for Piers and Michele

Heralding high festival, this late day
of sun is rising blue and silver. Not
knowing signs and omens, yet we may
like ancient Romans prognosticate now what
a life and life (two lives being one) will grow
and give: the other always there, unseen
or seen, roots quietly intertwined that know
no separation while, above, the green
stems are strong and most themselves. Though today
is shining some weathers shake the water
of the lake here, now so glossed with smoothest day,
but its depths stay still: you keep in touch with laughter
and love and stillness in the depths of you
and share a life that's always springing new.

ADELAÏDE AND THE DAFFODILS
(on hearing Beethoven's song)

The energy of words and of the voice's rising
is the insistent yellow and all but singing
(the day thrusting now and vigorous)

of daffodils against the still winter
browns and dark evergreens and the perennial shed.
Articulate they throw colour to the water,

cluttered surface of the pond below.
Thus reflected in water was the loved image
of Adelaïde, her lover's high

reach of music driving all thought.
And we, feeling after the awakened images that
overlie the clutter and drift of days,

receive the pushy, unquenchable colours,
juggling and jostling with words, early and late,
creating assertive seasons of light.

BREATH IS FIRE

On the hill's ridge hailstones will not melt:
they are imprisoned in frozen ponds,
balls of intense white. I kick
the solid water with the heavy heel
of my boot, chipping sparks of ice.

In *Flight into Egypt* Gentile da Fabriano
painted brown hills flanked by lemon trees;
Joseph turns to coax the donkey
over stony ground – the picture
on the Christmas card on which you wrote
your poem on the pervasiveness of love.

I kick a frozen pond watched
by four wild horses on the hilltop
stock still with the immobility of art or death.
But their breath is fire, its smoke streaming
into the jagged air of the frozen season.

WHO LOVES FIRST

I was speaking of a children's game
but "who loves first" was what you thought I'd said,
and we imagined love's eager contests,
prizes and penalties, possession and loss.
But as we walked at the sea line
we played our own love games:
"Peter loves Daphne" and "Daphne loves Peter
equally" we scratched in the sand
with stones, throwing our stones to fall
in the sea together. Then you gave me
a stone inscribed "With all my love":
grey with freckles and whirls of white,
grey merging into white, a smooth oval
full of speech and silence.

Now dark comes slowly but the late light
is fluent still and the potent rays
explode from black cloud to be trapped
by the Tyrrhenian Sea: the splash and gush
of light compels our sight. Everywhere
gestures of being persuade us; the black jetty
and its silhouettes mastering the dusk – a fishing line,
a gesticulating man, a couple entwined –
are extensions of our loving. The near hills
are impoverished black, the far
a deeper rose than sky, that patch of sky beyond
a seamless opulence of light.